NETWORKING
Made Easy

Patty Marler ■ Jan Bailey Mattia

VGM Career Horizons
NTC/Contemporary Publishing Company

Library of Congress Cataloging-in-Publication Data

Marler, Patty.
    Networking made easy / Patty Marler and Jan Bailey Mattia.
        p.   cm.
    ISBN 0-8442-4342-6
    1. Business networks. I. Mattia, Jan Bailey II. Title.
HD69.S8M328   1997
650.1'3—dc21   97-15798
                                                                CIP

*This project started as a dream ... quite simply, an idea.
It turned into a series of books and a friendship
that will last a lifetime.*

*Chase your dreams, whatever they may be—the universe
wants to work with you, you must only begin.*

Cover photograph copyright © Peter Correz/Tony Stone Images

Published by VGM Career Horizons
An imprint of NTC/Contemporary Publishing Company
4255 West Touhy Avenue, Lincolnwood (Chicago), Illinois 60646-1975, U.S.A.
Copyright © 1998 by NTC/Contemporary Publishing Company
All rights reserved. No part of this book may be reproduced, stored in a retrieval
system, or transmitted in any form or by any means, electronic, mechanical,
photocopying, recording or otherwise, without the prior permission of
NTC/Contemporary Publishing Company.
Manufactured in the United States of America
International Standard Book Number: 0-8442-4342-6
15 14 13 12 11 10 9 8 7 6 5 4 3 2 1

Contents

47

Introduction   1 ....

Special Features   2 ....

Networking Is ...   3 ....

Chapter 1: The Power of Networking   4 ....

    Six Degrees of Separation   5
    The Mathematics of It All   9
    The Power of Positive Energy   12
        Checking Your Reflection   15
        Learn to Say Yes   18

New Age Networking   21 ....

Chapter 2: You Are Your Own Business   23

Creatures of Habit   26

Walking the Walk   28

Thinking the Thought   30

Talking the Talk   31

    Reading Between the Lines   33

You, Your Business, and the Internet   36

Chapter 3: Fundamentals of Networking   38

Ready, Set, Go!   38

    Networking Within   39

    Extracurricular Contacts   41

Searching for Opportunities   41

The Etiquette of Networking   42

    Knowing Who to Talk To   44

    Connecting with People   46

    Speaking with Confidence   49

    Maintaining a Positive Outlook   50

    Listening and Following Through   52

    Notes of Appreciation   54

    Networking: A Two-Way Street   55

    Practice   56

    In Summary   56

Schmooze without Sleaze   57

Summary   59

Chapter 4: Networking Know-How   60

Opening-Line Bloopers   60

Saying it Right   61

    The Right Way ... Is There One?   61

    Introductions   62

    Social vs. Business Talk   64

    Topics for Discussion   68

    Networking Scenarios   68

Volunteering   73

    Timing   76

    Identifying Opportunities   78

    Approaching Employers   79

    Volunteer Networking   81

    Leaving Permanent Reminders   82

    In Summary   83

Maintaining Active Contacts   84

    The Usual Probes   85

    Creative Management   87

Conclusion   89

Introduction

Networking—the process of meeting people, developing a positive rapport, and encouraging people to help you—is a required skill in today's world. Helping others and requesting their assistance is perfectly acceptable and necessary. We all rely on others to a degree in our lives and this is a healthy social practice.

Networking Made Easy will describe what it takes to be an effective networker. We will look at the impact networking can have on your life and your search for employment. Considering yourself a "marketable business" will provide a different perspective to your networking and will help you see how you can market yourself in the same manner that companies promote their products.

The basics you need before you begin networking are described in "Fundamentals of Networking," and ideas and suggestions for effective networking are described in "Networking Know-How."

Networking is an exciting and rewarding experience. Once you discover its many benefits you will continue networking and it will become a way of life.

"Act as if it were impossible to fail."
—Dorothea Brande

Special Features

Special features throughout the book will help you pick out key points and discover new things about yourself and others.

 Notes clarify text with concise explanations.

 Helpful Hints provide ideas and suggestions to improve your networking potential.

 Business Brains provide ideas to keep you current and marketable in a demanding business world.

 Perspective Checks encourage you to look at your attitudes and feelings towards a variety of issues and challenge you to see other points of view.

 Life Bytes are condensed stories of real people who networked their way into some success.

 Special Thoughts provide inspiration and motivation.

It's time to greet your potential!

Networking Is . . .

People constantly talk about networking and describe how important it is, especially when looking for work. But what exactly is it?

Networking is simply a different way of looking at people and your relationships with them. Networking is:

✔ having something in common with another and discussing it.

✔ leaving a positive, lasting impression on others.

✔ helping people.

✔ establishing a connection with others.

✔ encouraging others to help you.

✔ done for both business and pleasure.

✔ getting in touch with others.

✔ socializing. Getting to know people and having them learn about you.

✔ the words you say, how you say them, your facial expression, and your body language.

✔ developing and utilizing friendships and acquaintances.

✔ fun.

✔ done every day, whether you recognize it or not.

"Production is not the application of tools to materials, but logic to work."

—Peter Drucker

Chapter 1

The Power of Networking

"Talents are best nurtured in solitude: character is best formed in the stormy billows of the world."

—Johann Von Goethe

Networking … the latest buzzword. You've heard it a million times before and now you're going to read it … "you gotta learn to network if you wanna get anywhere!"

Effective networking can get you a job, a date, a great deal on a new car, or an invitation to the grand opening of the hottest new club in town. Whatever you need, want, or think you need or want, someone you know, or the friend of the person you know, has it, or knows someone who knows how to get it. Whew! Sound confusing and complicated? Well, perhaps in writing it does, in practice, it is something we all do, every day whether we choose to call it networking or not.

For example, some friends of ours are getting married this year and, like everyone else, they are trying to make the whole event affordable. In keeping with that idea, we sat down the other day to make a list of all the things they would need to organize: hall, catering, flowers, photography … that sort of thing. Now, how, exactly, does this prove that we all network every day? Well, the next step in the whole procedure was to begin to brainstorm about who we knew.

- Who do we know that works in a hotel that could get us a deal on a space for a dance?

- Do we know someone who belongs to a private club that is big enough for a reception?

- Do we know a photographer that would trade pictures for some service we could offer (the groom is a carpenter)?

... you're getting the idea. We were at the beginning stages of networking, the "who do we know" that can help us stage.

Think about it. You've done it, you do it, probably more regularly than you think. Suddenly, however, when it comes to something like finding employment, we all forget that we have networked before and it didn't hurt us. In fact, more than likely, networking probably helped us get where we wanted to go. Take some time to think about situations where you networked effectively and try to apply those same techniques to your current situation.

 In case you're curious, the wedding is still a go, but we quickly realized we need to get out more and meet some new people!

Now, consider these thoughts on the power of networking.

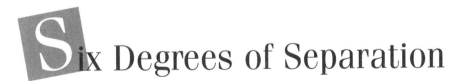

Six Degrees of Separation

A theory exists that suggests every individual in the world is separated from any other individual by only six people.

What?

Well, in other words, this idea implies you could meet and get to know everyone in the world simply by being introduced to six people, the first one being someone you know.

For example: Your friend Anton introduces you to his distant, long lost cousin Simon, who just moved to town and would like to join your soccer team. While you two are chatting and getting to know one another, Simon mentions that he used to play soccer for a great team. They had a phenomenal goal keeper that played with them, and you bear a striking resemblance to him. His name was Chris. Chris, incidentally, is now working in Thailand teaching English. All this is very interesting so far, don't you think?

Never decide ahead of time, "oh, how could they possibly help me," the possibilities are endless.

Well, Chris knows Lee, who happens to work in the kitchen at the Palace of the royal family of Thailand. (Chris and Lee are still playing soccer and play together twice a week.) Now conveniently enough, and it really isn't that unusual, the royal family in Thailand happens to know, and are close personal friends with, Lady Diana Spencer, the former Princess of Wales. Indeed, this is all simply fascinating, don't you think? But what on earth does it have to do with you out playing soccer in the rain in Vancouver half way around the world?

"Life has to be lived forward but can only be understood backward."

—Kierkegaard

Well, interestingly enough, you happen to volunteer for an organization that grants wishes to terminally ill children. It's a great organization, and you enjoy the work you do there. This week things are a little stressful for you, though. It's Thursday night, soccer night, and you find yourself telling Simon about this great little boy you're getting to know. His name is Mitch, he's eight years old, and he has inoperable brain cancer. There really is no certainty of how long he may live, and your organization would like to grant him a wish.

Now, you're expecting Mitch will want to take his family to Disneyland or play hockey with Wayne Gretzky, but he tells you he would like to meet a real, honest-to-goodness Princess, Princess Diana. You, of course, have no idea how you're going to begin to orchestrate this one, and in a relatively short period of time. Simon empathizes with your situation, but there is really nothing he can do for you.

Or is there?

Coincidentally, that same Thursday is also Simon's friend Chris's birthday (you know, the one in Thailand), and Simon gives him a call later that night to wish him a happy one. They chat about life and about soccer and, of course, you come up (because as you remember, you remind Simon of Chris … are you keeping up?) and so does your Princess problem. Simon hangs up the phone—Chris did have a great birthday, in case you're wondering, and that's the end of it …?

You must continue to put your thoughts, ideas, and needs out there. People can and will help you.

The next day is Friday, and Chris and his Thai friend Lee are playing soccer that weekend in a tournament. The team meets for a light practice Friday night and heads out for a team dinner after. Naturally it gets out that yesterday was Chris's birthday, and everyone wishes him well, and he remembers the conversation he had with Simon. He mentions to Lee that his buddy from Canada called him and tells him also of the story of Mitch, the little boy with cancer.

As you're starting to see a distinct pattern here, you can well imagine what happens next.

You guessed it. Sunday night after the tournament Lee can't celebrate with the team because he's needed at work to meet with the head cook about a special dinner the royal family is planning. Apparently this dinner is a big deal because the King pops in to see how things are coming along. As it would happen, Lee is a skilled pastry chef and the King has a special request for dessert he would like to pass on to Lee personally. In passing, the King asks Lee how the soccer tournament went, and they begin to chat. And … yes, the story of Mitch and the Princess dilemma comes into the conversation.

Take pride in becoming a good conversationalist and a great story-teller. You never know who you may be appealing to.

Well, the royal dinner is a smashing success, the dessert is a sensation and once again it's Thursday. You're just heading out the door to soccer practice once again, and your phone rings. It's long distance, from London of all places. Monique is on the line, and she is the media representative and event coordinator for, you guessed it, Princess Diana. She unknowingly asks to speak with Mitch—you really can't blame her for being confused after all the times this story has changed hands!

Once you get your mouth closed and catch your breath you quickly explain to her who you are, who Mitch is, and what it is your organization does. She seems quite receptive and knows that this type of thing is in line with much of the charity work Princess Diana does ... indeed, it sounds promising. As a matter of fact, Diana will be in the country for a function later that month, and you are left with a phone number to contact Monique to arrange a suitable time for Diana and Mitch to meet. This has taken exactly a week and frankly, you don't care that you are now half an hour late for soccer practice.

Sound a little far-fetched? Is it? Maybe you should take up soccer!

This is a good time to remember how small the world is. You never know who the people you are talking to are related to, good friends with, or business associates of.

Seriously, think about it. It really isn't that much of a stretch of the imagination to think that we could meet someone in any of the farthest reaches of the globe. Today, so many of us, our friends, family, and acquaintances are traveling, working, and living abroad.

So, with that thought in mind, think of the possibilities of meeting people who could help you with your job search! Six degrees of separation ... hey, even if it's eight ... think of the potential!

"Ships in harbor are safe, but that's not what ships are built for."

—John Shedd

The Mathematics of It All

Six degrees of separation is a very interesting thought with unlimited potential, but perhaps it is a little "out there" for you. Let's take a look at the power of networking from a mathematical perspective.

Let's suppose for a second you've opened a small deli in a trendy little area downtown. Business is slow, but you're new and you have faith in the advertising you've done. It happens to be Tuesday, and your best friend Yvonne has just come back into town after an extended business trip so you invite her down for lunch. She hasn't seen the new place, but she was around for some of the planning and certainly for all of the dreaming.

Granted, you're a little nervous about her opinion and wonder if you were ready to invite her, but ... she loves it—from the food to the service to the flower arrangements in the washrooms, she loves it all. If it hadn't been Tuesday and there wasn't a staff meeting she had to attend, Yvonne would, in fact, have loved to while the afternoon away drinking wine with you and catching up on all the news since she's been gone. Unfortunately for her (but fortunately for you, as we will soon see), she heads back to work.

On any first meeting of even a "sort of" business nature, be sure your first impression is a professional, positive, and long-lasting one—it may be passed on to several people.

So, Pat happens to be sitting at the front desk when Yvonne walks into the office after lunch. Oddly enough, he doesn't have the phone attached to his ear like he usually does, and he takes the opportunity to welcome Yvonne back to the office and ask her how she's been. Well, the business trip was long, sort of productive, the weather was horrid, her husband missed her, and the dog got sick while she was away. She also tells Pat she has just come from the greatest little place where she had the most fabulous lunch she has had in a while. As a matter of fact, Yvonne happily launches into quite a glowing review of your restaurant and makes Pat promise he'll try it for lunch before the end of the week. Naturally Pat promises with a laugh, knowing Yvonne will hold him to it (one new customer for you), and reaches for the phone as it starts to ring.

Trust your product—you, and remember: If you represent yourself in a positive professional manner, so will your friends when they speak of you.

Now, not five minutes later Ray comes by with a new client he needs to impress. Lunch is in order, they've been hard at work negotiating a deal all morning—great food, great atmosphere, great price, and somewhere funky that the client has never been. Well, Pat, feeling the pressure of the moment, but knowing he's up to it, remembers Yvonne's enthusiastic recommendation of your restaurant and passes it along to Ray. Off they go for lunch (two more customers for you).

It turns out, much to your credit, that both Ray and his client very much enjoy lunch at your deli, and they don't hesitate to tell people where they stopped for lunch. As a matter of fact, they happen to each tell five friends about your restaurant and away it goes from there.

"The best preparation for tomorrow is to do today's work superbly well."

—Sir William Osler

This is where the math part comes in and the numbers really kick into high gear. If Ray and his client each tell five friends and each of those ten tell five friends, suddenly you have yourself a huge lunch rush and whole restaurant full of new customers just by inviting one friend. What are the exact numbers? Well, you've had 54 people in for lunch, just because your friend liked what you had done with the place and told someone about it. Imagine what would happen if each of those 54 people brought a spouse, a coworker, or a friend from the office down the street with them for lunch!

This is truly the power of networking!

So what did you learn from this little math drill? Well, for one thing, instead of inviting one friend next time, you'll have the first day of business dedicated to all your friends, feeding and impressing them so they head out and tell all their friends about your business. The bigger the number you start with, the bigger the number you'll serve in your deli. Business will surely boom!

"The past should be a spring-board, not a hammock."

—Ivern Ball

Remember: You are networking when you ask someone where he bought his great jacket, if he happens to know a good restaurant in town, or if she can recommend a good movie to see or book to read, who cuts her hair, or who sold her house. You are a social creature. You come into contact with new people every day, sometimes you chat with them and sometimes you don't, but if you do, chances are there is some form of networking going on.

LB

Dean is an extraordinary athlete, and always has been. His official claim to fame is his ability on the trampoline, having competed on an international level, but anything else he tries he's good at. For fun, in his spare time, Dean took on the job of mascot for a local football team. He loved the job, he got to perform in front of people, use his trampoline skills, and be as silly as he wanted to be for the entire game. In Dean's second year as a mascot, the NBA came to town with a new team, lots of money and all the advertising hype that comes with it. They were looking for entertainer/athlete types who could perform at half time and between the quarters to keep the fans' energy level up—but, sadly, Dean never heard about auditions and the squad was formed without him. However, a few games into the season, the basketball entertainers decided they needed a little spice in their performance and started to chat amongst themselves about who could help them. Someone mentioned he had seen Dean at a football game, and it would be great if they could get him. Too bad no one knew who it was in the suit. To make a long story short, the squad members started asking their friends, and a friend of a friend of a friend (that's only three degrees of separation away!) knew it was Dean and gave them his number. The job was his if he wanted it.

The Power of Positive Energy

Have you ever noticed that when you're in a good mood people seem to be drawn to you? They walk up and talk to you whether you look at them or not, whether you smile and open conversation with them or not, or whether you even want them to or not! Positive energy seems to attract people, and you find yourself meeting new people whether you intended to … or not. It's very similar to when you get a great haircut and you love the way you look, or you're wearing a brand new suit and the tailoring is divine—you look great, you feel great, and people notice you. You often have people come up to you and ask you where you got that suit or haircut.

A lot of this is about confidence.

LB

Martin is an actor. Well, actually, Martin wants to be an actor and he is willing to work hard in an industry filled with beautiful people and temperamental executives. It happened to be a sunny day in an otherwise rainy week and, taking full advantage of the situation, Martin headed out on his inline skates for some sun and some exercise. Forty-five minutes later Martin was in the area of a film and TV studio that was always busy casting various projects. On a whim he skated by. There was a man outside having a smoke, and Martin paused to have a look through the front doors at what was going on inside. He smiled a hello at the man, who smiled back and asked if Martin was an actor looking for an audition. Martin, not knowing who he was speaking with, said yes he was an actor, but he wasn't auditioning, and asked if the man was working there today. The older gentleman laughed and said he was, in fact, casting a television movie there and asked if his assistant had a copy of Martin's resume. Not a guaranteed job for Martin, but closer to one than earlier that day. In the end it turned out the older gentleman was, in fact, a prominent casting director Martin had been trying to reach by phone!

So, you're confident with your suit—you know you look great, or you love your new haircut and it gives you some added confidence that day. So you like who you are and people can feel that from you, and somehow this is going to help you network to get a job? Still a little too vague for you?

OK, think about the saying that suggests it's easier to find a job when you have a job. Why is that? Personal power, positive energy, and the power of self-confidence. You feel, consciously or not, you are in a position of strength because you aren't searching for work. Maybe you have a great job, maybe you just have an adequate job, the point is you feel confident you have an answer to that frustratingly common question, "So, what do you do for a living?"

If you have trouble with the "What do you do?" question, spend some time coming up with an answer that is comfortable for you.

You may think that is the most ridiculous thing you've heard in a long time, but think about it before you dismiss it. If there has ever been a time in your life when you have been looking for work, answer honestly:

1. Have you ever paused while you were filling out a form and it asked for your occupation?

2. Have you ever had to stop and think when asked for your work phone number?

Or,

3. Have you, on maybe one occasion, not wanted to go to a party where you knew you would have to meet new people and the first thing that would come out of their mouths was *that* question?

Did you answer honestly? If you did, you know what an effect not working can have on your self-confidence.

"Our doubts are traitors
And make us lose the good we oft might win
By fearing to attempt."

—Shakespeare

Why?

Well, for a lot of reasons, most of them having to do with social pressure and the value we as a society place on work. Because of this social pressure, we often feel as though only when we're working are we valuable, contributing members of society, with something to do everyday, and something to talk about at parties.

The point is, when you are working, you are not self-conscious about not working, you do not find yourself coughing before you mention you are in-between jobs, and that gives you confidence. Suddenly you feel more qualified to discuss future job and market trends with someone you may or may not know who is starting up a new company. Who knows? Based on your engaging conversation, that person may indeed ask where you are currently working and if you've considered a move!

Take advantage of the networking opportunities that come your way when you are employed, and keep in touch with the connections you make. You never know when you'll need them.

Perhaps you are more confident meeting new people and discussing your ideas for advertising on the Internet. Why? Because at this point they are just ideas and you don't feel like you are desperately pitching your ideas to someone in a position to hire you. Finally, you are simply more confident putting yourself in places where there are people with the power, influence, and ability to hire you for your skills, when those skills and abilities are currently being used and valued by some organization—when you have a job.

Checking Your Reflection

So how does this help you now? Well, if you currently have a job, consciously take a look at how you act when you are in group situations. Evaluate the way you speak with others about your job, your field, and your expertise. Are you more comfortable and confident discussing things you know? Or are you equally as confident outside your comfort zone? Take a few notes to help you remember those feelings of confidence and personal power … just in case you want to start looking for a new career soon or you are forced to start looking for a new career soon.

LB

Lorna is a working accountant. She is looking for a change even though her job has been quite interesting recently. Lorna has been researching the feasibility of her company investing in and developing a new golf course. She has done some extensive traveling to talk with experts in the field and has spoken with many companies who are currently developing properties or who are planning to in the near future. She put considerable time and effort into the project and was proud of the result. Indeed, so was the company she works for, and they decided to go ahead with the project. Where did that leave Lorna? Well, as I mentioned, the company was so impressed with her effort they put her in charge of purchasing equipment, hiring contractors to develop the site, and generally to oversee the project. Lorna put together quotes, manuals, financial projections, and all sorts of terms and agreements on paper and over the phone. Along the way, she made sure everyone she dealt with knew her name and that her name was on everything she put down on paper. Why? Lorna quit her job after the development was underway and went back to school. The program she chose is mostly at night, enabling her to find a job during the day. Well, the phone rang a week or two after school started, and it was one of those companies she had contacted when researching her golf course project. It turns out they were beginning development on their project soon and wondered if Lorna would be interested in doing some contract work. They had read some of the literature she put together and talked to a few people, and decided she was the person they wanted at the foundation of their project. Looks like Lorna won't have to worry about a student loan after all!

Well, this is all just lovely, isn't it? You don't currently have a job, so what has this got to do with you? If you are currently looking for work or a change of scenery in your career, think about how you act in situations where you could be networking with others for employment.

- Honestly ask yourself if it bothers you to state what your employment status is and what your future objectives are.

Or,

- Do you completely avoid those types of questions that would take a conversation in that direction?

- Are you uncomfortable fielding comments about where the world of work is going, or do you simply avoid those types of situations altogether?

If you answered "yes" to those questions, you are seriously limiting your ability to use the power of networking. You must thoroughly immerse yourself in situations—both social and business—where you can meet people who can help you with your career path. If you are uncomfortable with these situations do the following: rehearse them, think back to the time when you were working, and honestly try to evaluate if you are a different person, or if you feel like a different person because you are not working. Consciously or not, a lack of confidence because of a temporary lack of employment can seriously affect how others view you.

Remember you are not alone in all of this. Many of the people you meet have been unemployed or know someone who is.

LB

Vhing is a friend of mine. Ever since I've known him he has been trying to break into the music business, and lately things haven't been going so well. After much soul searching, he has decided maybe he wasn't meant to be a rock 'n roll star, and he should look for something else. He doesn't have any postsecondary education, and music is all he's ever done other than his recent compulsion to travel and see the world. Well, he and I sat down one night and did a little brainstorming and came up with what we think is a pretty good option for Vhing, incorporating his need for change and his love of travel. It just so happened that I was recently chatting with a long-time friend of mine who works in the hospitality industry in South Africa. He is in charge of hiring and training guides for the large game reserve he works on and is having some trouble finding quality people. Vhing, as far as I am concerned, is "quality people," and I certainly didn't hesitate handing over that South African phone number to him. So, the music business has lost a great songwriter for now, but South Africa and its wildlife have gained an outgoing, energetic tour guide.

Networking is a powerful tool if only you begin to use it. In a business world where competition is increasing and companies are finding themselves faced with budget and staffing cuts, it is important to employers to hire people who are multifaceted, good at their jobs, and good at working in small, cohesive, productive groups. This means employees with great customer service skills and excellent people skills are great assets. By surrounding yourself with people who are in business, or are in the market for positive, goal-oriented, results people, you are immediately increasing your odds at finding suitable employment for yourself. Now, add to that formula your enthusiasm, energy, and ideas and you have some very interesting conversations and probably some interesting opportunities for networking and meeting like-minded people.

 Surrounding yourself and talking with positive people may not always land you an immediate job, but you can be guaranteed it will boost your confidence and you will find people who support your growth and your direction.

Learn to Say Yes

Because of what not working can do to self-confidence levels, it is sometimes easy to fall into the "no" routine.

What?

In other words, *more than ever when you are not working it is important to get out and meet people.* However, sometimes unknowingly, it is easy to start to routinely say "no" to your friends, family, past business associates, and potential new business associates when they do ask you to come out with them. For various reasons, when you aren't working, there is a tendency to begin to withdraw from people:

Why?

- You may be depressed.

- You may be self-conscious about not working.

- You may begin to think people are only feeling sorry for you.

- You may be on a tight budget.

Whatever your reasons, it is normal to find yourself saying "no" to opportunities to go out and meet new people or even old acquaintances. Break the routine!

Think about this: "No" has a tendency to create stress in our lives. Generally, we have some trouble saying "no," especially to our friends, without offering them an excuse or reason why we can't see them.

This creates, you guessed it, stress. So, don't say "no"—save yourself some of the agony!

 Pay attention to how many times you say "no" in the next week. Look at the situations where you are more prone to using the "no" word. Is there a pattern?

Begin today to practice saying "yes." Saying "yes" to a variety of situations, offers, changes, and possibilities says "yes" to an unlimited number of opportunities. Quit resisting the power you have to create opportunity for yourself. Start saying "yes" to the things that are trying to come your way. You may be surprised by the events that begin to take place and the "chances" that occur.

 "You can't steal second base and keep one foot on first."

—Unnamed 60-year-old Junior Executive

Although it seems like networking is simply a trendy buzzword for people who want to sound "hip," it really is a solid tool for your job search. You've heard about it a million times, and you will hear about it a million more until you actually begin to do it consciously.

It is a trendy word, but it is a trendy word for something people do naturally and have been doing for a long time. Unfortunately, often when something is given a definition and added to the invisible list of things one must learn to be successful in life … we are suddenly unsure of how to go about it and afraid we may fail. Remember, at some point, everyone is uncomfortable networking, you are not alone in that. Fear is not a bad thing when you are faced with a new or unfamiliar situation. There is, however, an underlying feeling of helplessness when one is afraid. It is far better to push on through your fear than to live with the continuing, underlying feeling of helplessness.

Ultimately, what makes the difference between people who are master networkers and reap the rewards and those who do not? The masters acknowledge their fear, understand that sometimes it is inevitable, and then they go out and do it anyway!

 We guarantee you will feel better about yourself, stronger and more confident if you acknowledge your fear of networking and go out and conquer it. There is nowhere to go but ahead!

New Age Networking

There is a new way of thinking and viewing the world that is creeping into mainstream Western thinking. Whether you agree with, believe in, or subscribe to these new ideas, you may at least find them interesting. Fundamentally, we are becoming a society filled with people who find themselves searching for something, some sense of higher purpose, some reason for doing the things they do, in an ever-evolving, fast-paced society filled more and more with work, work, and more work.

As ancient Eastern thought slowly begins to sneak into our Western culture we are seeing a new breed of business people. At the root of these new ideas is the thought, or founding belief, that indeed, everything happens for a reason. If we adopt this philosophy as our own, we may begin to look at networking in a slightly different manner. Consider:

- Everything does happen for a reason, the good and the bad, you simply have to look to see how the pieces fit with your life and your direction.

- You are never a victim of life. If you take responsibility for everything that occurs in your life, even things that seem like setbacks, and don't simply look for others to blame because it is easier, only then will you progress beyond those situations in the direction you are meant to go.

- You will make a decision, and the universe will find a way to test you to see if that decision is one you are sure of.

- You will draw situations—again, good and bad—people, and opportunities to yourself in order to learn and increase your understanding of the world and of people.

- Learning to listen to and trust your instincts will be the greatest business skill you learn.

- If your instinct tells you to go to a party, meeting, or some other type of function that you really don't want to go to … go. You will meet someone or learn something that will help you with your search.

- What goes around does come around. Make a positive difference in someone's day today. It will come back to you.

- If you are headed in the right direction, you will feel calm and focused. If you are not, or you stray from your path, you will feel confused, unfocused, and scattered.

- There really are no wrong decisions. Whatever you do and which-ever direction you take, you will learn something and you will grow because of it.

- Material things are not what matters—caring about those around you and becoming happy with who you are and what you do—these are things that are important, and people are beginning to change their lives accordingly.

"It is only with the heart that one can see rightly; what is essential is invisible to the eye."

—The Little Prince

Chapter 2

You Are Your Own Business

"Men go abroad to wonder at the
heights of mountains, at the huge
waves of the sea, at the long
courses of the rivers, at the vast
compass of the ocean, at the
circular motion of the stars,
and they pass themselves by
without wonder."

—St. Augustine

You, as a person, an employable person with skills and abilities, are a
business. When you are searching for employment that is suitable to
you and your wants and needs, you must consider yourself a business
with a product, assets, liabilities, a niche in the marketplace, and the
need to move with the times or lose out to your competitors.

When you are working at finding a job you must become your own
small business. No, you don't have to see a lawyer, start a corporation,
pay yourself dividends, and set out shareholder agreements, but you do
need to start to think of yourself as a viable, marketable, saleable, necessary small business.

What?

Consider if you were the deli owner we spoke of in the previous chapter:

How will you advertise your company?

What are your company assets?

What are your company drawbacks, shortcomings, or liabilities?

Who are your clients?

Who are your potential clients?

What makes your business special?

Why would people want to buy your product?

Do you provide better service than the company next door?

How long will there be a market for your product?

Is there room for expansion and diversification, and are you willing to do the work it would take?

In order to ensure there is a market for your deli and there will be customers to eat the great recipes that have been handed down in your family for generations, you will need to answer all these questions about your new business venture. There are a lot of delis out there, so you need to make sure you tell people yours is the best, that they hear that from other people, and when they come in, they get proof for themselves.

You have a vested interest in the "company," so be sure to investigate all the options. Take a look at some success stories, and see what strategies you can adopt for your own job search.

Now, these are exactly the things you need to consider with respect to yourself. You must think of yourself as the business and your skills and abilities as the product. What do *you* have to offer an employer (the customer) that other people (other businesses) do not. Ask yourself all of the same questions you would if you had just opened a retail store, a restaurant, a local garage, or a home-based business.

Take the time to research the market with yourself as the product the same as you would if your product were clothes, food, car parts, or computer graphics: Is there a market? Who are the consumers? and How do I get myself/my product in touch with those consumers?

Take a course in advertising, business, or marketing. Who knows what you might learn or who you might meet.

Thinking of your job search in this way may help you come up with some new and creative ways to market yourself:

- Write a mandate that encompasses your vision for your future.

- Outline your goals and objectives for the promotion of your business (you).

- Create innovative sales ideas and advertising packages for you, your business.

- List all the people you can think of who may need a product such as yours and then begin the process of calling and meeting with them to discuss your marketability.

- Research and learn about businesses that may be similar to yours. Find out if they are successful, why they are, and if they can be of some assistance to you.

- Objectively decide if your business is up-to-date with the trends and current needs of the job market, and do something about updating, if necessary.

- List the places you plan to target and initially focus your advertising on.

- Set up an office at home out of which you plan your "attack."

- Tell everyone you know and people you meet about your great business (you!) and all it has to offer.

 Remember, people are always willing to try a new product once. If they like it, they'll tell people they know. If they don't like it, they'll tell everyone, whether they know them or not! Make a favorable first impression.

Thinking of yourself as a small business may help you distance yourself from the sometimes emotional side effects of looking for work. You need to objectively think of your strengths and your weaknesses, and how you can improve them to make your product more saleable, more current. If your job search is not immediately successful you can rationally look at why your "company" was turned down and what the other "company" had to offer that you didn't. It is much more difficult and takes longer to get past the idea that something was "wrong with me."

When you are shopping for employment, look for lessons in what you do. What did you learn today, positive and negative, why did it happen, how can you make it happen again, or be certain it doesn't?

This may sound trivial to you, but when you take away some of the personal nature of the job search, you take away the feelings that you as a person are not good enough. You, as a person, are great! You are who you are, and your personal life is your personal life. Your business, however, may need some updating and some work, and that is fine. It is no reflection on your worth as a person or as a meaningful individual. When you do not receive a job offer you hoped for, you must remember, you personally are not being rejected, your business was simply inappropriate in some way for that position. It is up to you to find out what aspect of your business needs work and to do what is necessary to realign your "company."

"It's not what happens to you. It's what you do about it."

—W. Mitchell

Creatures of Habit

For better or for worse, most people are creatures of habit. Indeed, sometimes it does work out for the better and sometimes it does work out ... worse. If your day feels incomplete if you don't make it to the gym for at least 45 minutes, that is a great habit—if you make it a practice to tell your partner every day, at least once, how much he or she means to you, that is another great habit. But when it comes to networking and finding yourself employment, there are a few daily habits that can get in your way.

Whether you are working and looking for a change or simply keeping your options open, or whether you are currently not working, take a look at your lifestyle for some of the following patterns and how they can affect your networking success.

"Motivation is what gets you started. Habit is what keeps you going."

—Jim Ryun

What?

- You're working. It's your lunch hour and no matter what the weather, no matter what office function is going on, you sit alone and read your book.

  By doing a little socializing with the people at work you may find people who have similar interests. Who knows, you may branch off and start a small business on the side, or you may make a connection that will benefit you in the future.

- You ride the bus to work every day and every day you wear your walkman so people can't or won't speak to you.

  Not only are you missing out on the chance to say or receive a warm hello, you are missing countless opportunities to meet people who could greatly assist your job search.

- You practice your "don't talk to me" face in the mirror to use when you stand in line at the grocery store.

  It is said that the grocery store is the best place to be if you are looking for a potential romantic mate. If you can make those kind of relationships happen there, it's got to be a great place to strike up business relationships!

- You never go to company functions that take place outside of work unless absolutely required to … "the company gets too much of my time during the week."

  Depending on the size of your organization, there may certainly be people you have not met. Additionally, you never know whose guest at an after-work function may turn out to be a great business contact for you in the future.

- You *never* read the newspaper or watch the news because it's too depressing.

  Yes, the news can become depressing, particularly if you aren't working and the news is about layoffs. You do need to keep current, however. So, stay away from the daily paper, but perhaps pick up the weekend edition. You never know what helpful tidbit you'll find!

- You don't own a computer, and you definitely want nothing to do with that Internet!

  *Well, fear of rapidly advancing technology is very common, and the Internet and talk of it is certainly advancing rapidly. Unfortunately, there really is no way around this one. You **will** be affected by this technology. So, you can go out there, learn about it, use it, and benefit from it, or you can bury your head in the sand and hope the technology can't find you.*

 Let yourself be afraid, be nervous, be tense … it's energy, learn to convert it into something useful— action!

So, habits can be a good thing, or they can be a bad thing. Take an honest look at yours—better yet, get someone you trust and respect to help you look at your habits and see where they are helping or hindering the sale of your business (your job search).

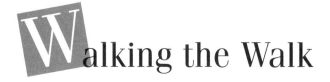alking the Walk

Like any game, sport, or even any new hobby, networking is a skill. If you want to be any good at it and you want your business to succeed, you absolutely must practice. This means:

1. **Go out of your way to meet people**—You don't feel like going to a birthday party tonight, you have nothing to wear, and there is a great movie on TV. Get off the couch and go! You never know who you'll meet, and odds are you will have a great time.

2. **Remember the names of people you meet**—It doesn't do you much good to get out and meet people if you don't remember who they are. Practice remembering names, write them down, get a business card, and pass out yours … do whatever it takes.

3. **Take a genuine interest in people and what their interests are**—Networking is not offensive. It does not mean being slick and smooth and manipulating people to get what you want. That may work once, perhaps even twice, but it won't take long for people to see through you and word will get around.

Be patient.

4. **Keep in touch with new friends and old acquaintances**—We live in an ever changing world. People move, change jobs, and are constantly meeting new people. By keeping in touch with people you are keeping your business in touch with their networks of contacts as well.

5. **Listen actively when you are involved in any conversation**—There is nothing worse than chatting with someone who is only interested in one thing in the conversation—"How can you help me?" Be an active participant in conversations. You may meet someone interesting, and conversation may move in any number of unexpected directions. You never know what people have to offer unless you listen.

Don't be afraid to talk about your ideas, dreams, and hopes. By doing so, you will draw supporters to yourself and you will help clarify your intentions.

Thinking the Thought

Now that you are actively and faithfully doing your part networking, it's time to be aware that more than half the battle of the networking game is played in your mind. You've probably figured this one out already because it can sometimes be a genuine battle to get yourself up off the couch to go out somewhere, or even to go into your office to pick up the phone. What in the world is going on?

"Nothing lasts forever—not even your troubles."

—Arnold H. Glasow

Well, you know your business is worth something to any employer who will take the time to give you and your skills a chance. However, as you start to get out there and meet people, you may not meet with instant success. As a result, you might start to question your confidence and your abilities: Perhaps I'm not in demand. Perhaps my skills aren't as great as I thought. You may think, I doubt there is anyone out there who is willing to help me find work. Okay, that's more than enough, *stop* right there!

This horrible, irritating noise you're hearing is your mental mouthpiece talking, and you must know, there are times when it talks incessantly. The worst part is, it usually says negative things unless you make an effort to teach it otherwise. The mouthpiece can make us wonder if we really can do what we set out to do. Is my business marketable? Will my partner approve? Will people like me when I meet them? and so on.

So how do you counteract this ridiculous little noise in your head?

✔ the first step is to simply be aware of it—accept it for what it is, nervous energy that is temporarily misguided.

✔ surround yourself with positive and supportive people who let you know you are doing well.

✔ know that nothing you do, no decision you make is wrong, you will learn something and readjust your course if necessary.

✔ tell the mouthpiece every day as you shave or brush your teeth that you are going to be successful with or without its help—so it might as well say something positive.

Remember, you as a person are a business. Obviously you wouldn't let someone say horrible, negative, unfounded things about your new deli, or your new garage, so why on earth would you tolerate negative comments from yourself about yourself!

"Forgiveness is a gift we give ourselves."

—Anonymous

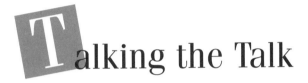alking the Talk

You are your business, and you wouldn't dream of hiring anything but the most professional people to represent you as a business, would you? So, do you qualify as the most professional of people representing you/your business?

Much of a first impression is created as soon as we open our mouths, so it is interesting and informative to listen closely to our choice of words and the way we speak. Often when we are speaking to others we are simply thinking out loud, and things may not necessarily come out as we hoped. Similarly, we often assume because we are using words and thought patterns we are comfortable with and know the meaning of, those we're speaking with will naturally understand the message we are trying to get across. This is not necessarily so!

"We don't know who we are until we see what we can do."

—Martha Grimes

people don't understand you because you know what you're saying (do)

Unfortunately, many words in the English language have more than one meaning, and even more importantly, many words suggest certain things about you and your character when you use them. For example, we all know people we would consider calling "whiners." Not a nice term, but when you say the word it brings to mind a very specific picture of a particular person.

31

What?

The term suggests someone who speaks with a definite sound quality to his or her voice, and uses phrases like, "Why does this always happen to me," or, "I never knew," or "Nobody told me," and so forth.

Try again. Think of someone you would consider arrogant or snobbish. You immediately hear a certain quality in this person's voice, perhaps even picture him or her standing in a particular way. What kind of phrases or words escape this person's lips? Perhaps things like, "I would never do that," or, "If you ask my opinion," or, "Oh, I've done that many times" may slip down his or her nose at you in conversations.

The point is, we all have a characteristic way of speaking that conveys a message to others of what kind of person we are and what kind of business we are involved in. Indeed, this might not be such a bad thing, but sometimes the image that comes across in certain situations is not really a true one. Another example: we all know people who are normally warm and friendly but who become shy and withdrawn in social situations. People think they are snobs or stuck up when the opposite is actually true.

 Take the time to use a cassette recorder, or better yet, a video camera on a few different occasions to capture yourself in social situations (or business ones if possible). Take an honest look at whether you talk the talk!

Each of us probably has a friend or two who are normally relaxed and easy going but become obnoxious and downright silly when around people they don't know well or those they feel they must impress … people quickly get tired of their antics. Or, we know those who are intelligent, confident people, who suddenly forget they speak the English language when asked to approach and meet someone for the first time—all that intelligence and confidence goes right out the window!

So you can see that sometimes first impressions can be terribly misleading and unforgiving. You need to be aware of the type of person you are and the "Mr. Hyde" you may turn into in public or high-pressure situations. If you have difficulty evaluating your public behavior, which most people do, have a close friend (someone supportive, not critical) help you with your observations.

You really must go into this with an open mind and a willingness to change. Otherwise you are just looking for stress.

Reading Between the Lines

Now, let's talk specifics when it comes to that first, all-important impression. Language. Not only do the words you choose to use in conversation say a lot about you to other people, they also subconsciously send a message to your own brain about the kind of person you are.

What?

Think about it. If you tell yourself often enough you are a poor public speaker, odds are you will be a poor public speaker. Why? Well, you've been telling yourself for so long you aren't any good at it that it will certainly be a challenge to even force yourself to try it, let alone practice. If you do finally get the nerve to open your mouth while in front of a group, again, you have told yourself for so long you aren't good at it that you are defeated before you even start—yes, you've created a mental block for yourself. Finally, if you do get up and speak and you are good at it, will you even believe it? What a mess! It is truly amazing what we can talk ourselves into or out of!

self fulfilling prophecy

 "We promise according to our hopes, and perform according to our fears."

—La Rochefoucauld

So, take some time to really listen to the way you talk, what you say about yourself and to yourself. Remember, you are representing your business, in fact, you may be the only representative of your business sometimes, so you must do a good job of it.

How?

Be on the lookout for phrases and words that suggest you lack confidence. Phrases like "I can't" suggest you are a victim, someone without the strength or initiative to change your situation if it needs changing. Remember, you always have a choice. Are you doing something because you choose to do it and will accept whatever consequences result? Or, are you involved in, or doing something simply because you fell into it and don't know how to get out?

Again, the words you use in everyday conversations are a pretty good indicator of how you perceive yourself.

 Remember, we are talking about you, the business, here. This is something you are doing to help your business. Take it seriously, but not personally.

Consider the following "victim" phrases and then the alternate "choice" phrases:

I can't　　**I won't**

- "I can't" says there is nothing you can do about it.

- "I won't" says you choose not to.

I should　　**I could**

- "I should" implies you don't want to, but guilt will make you.

- "I could" gives you the option if you choose to do so!

It's not my fault　　**I am totally responsible**

- "It's not my fault" says you are a victim with no control.

- "I am responsible" says you have the strength to make a change!

It's a problem   **This is an opportunity**

- "It's a problem" says it's negative and you'll have to dig your way out.

- "It's an opportunity" suggests challenge, excitement and energy!

Life is always so hard   **This is an exciting challenge**

- "Life is hard" implies you plod your way through, barely keeping up.

- "This is a challenge" says you take an active part in where you're going!

I hope   **I know**

- "I hope" says you can't really help what is going on, you just have to sit back and wait.

- "I know" says you will do whatever you need to to make it happen!

If only   **Next time**

- "If only" is a wistful wish that someone would do it for you so it would be easy.

- "Next time" says you will make changes and things will go the way you want them to!

… get the idea?

So, make an honest analysis of your speaking habits and decide, are you saying what you really want to say and sounding how you want to sound? Are you coming across as the independent-thinking, confident, business-minded individual you are? Do you hope you'll find a job, or do you *know* you'll find a job?

 Make a point of taking some time each day to visualize your success. See yourself in your new job, at your desk, in the boardroom, at the factory … wherever.

You, Your Business, and the Internet

As you are, no doubt, already aware, the Internet is the most talked about, fastest growing technology today. We are suddenly finding ourselves surrounded by talk of: the Web, the Net, chat rooms, e-mail, and virtual reality, a whole new technical vocabulary that was virtually unheard of five years ago. It is overwhelming, exciting, intimidating, and fascinating all at the same time.

So what does it mean to you? *Change.*

Whether you are currently employed, looking for full-time employment, or seeking contract work to do from home, you will find Internet technology creeping into your life. Your friends are giving you e-mail addresses to contact them, your kids are researching science and history projects on the Web, your neighbor is shopping for a car via the Net, and even the local sports pub has a Web site. This is a technology that will not be ignored. Even condominiums are now being built with their own fiber optic access to the Internet. You will be affected by this.

"The strongest principle of growth lies in human choice."

—George Elliot

If you are already confidently "surfing the Net" you know it is a wealth of information and a communication marvel. The potential is just starting to unfold. Right now the technology is advancing so quickly it is virtually impossible for anyone but the most devoted computer gurus to keep up with it. This does not mean, however, that you should wait for the smoke to clear before getting in the know! If you wait for that to happen you'll wait a long time and will find yourself so far behind you'll think you're ahead.

So why is it so important for you to keep up with Internet technology? For a number of reasons:

• Change is good for you, it keeps you active and on your toes.

• It won't be that long before your computer runs your home.

• Your kids are growing up on the Internet.

- The potential for communication and networking is only just beginning to be realized.

- Employers and individuals alike are only beginning to access the incredible pool of people and resources available on the Internet.

- Employers will post jobs on the Internet and be able to access candidate information from all over the world.

- Job candidates will be able to research companies and make connections on-line with people who can assist them in their job search.

- You will be able to chat with people on-line in the same industry as you, all over the world, and discover how they got where they are.

You're getting the idea of the potential here?

Take the time to do some investigative work of your own. Go to your local computer store, visit an Internet cafe, check out your local library, these are all places you can "play" on the Net with someone there to help you navigate successfully. Make it a priority on your list of things to do—you'll be glad you did.

You are learning to be a master networker, you're practicing every day, and you are definitely getting somewhere and making progress for yourself. The Internet is simply a tool to help you reach a bigger market, a tool to help you get where you want to go. Use it for what it is—you may be surprised at the result.

"They are able who think they are able."

—Virgil

If you do happen to stick your foot in your mouth when you're trying to meet and impress someone, don't be afraid to laugh and admit you're nervous. We are, after all, human.

Chapter 3

Fundamentals of Networking

Big business, little business, you. All businesses must do one thing if they are going to succeed—*Sell themselves*. Customers need to know about a business, its services and products before they can use them. Similarly, your customers (employers) need to know about the services you have to offer—your skills, expertise, and knowledge. It is up to you to promote your assets thoroughly and effectively.

"When the rock is hard, we get harder than the rock. When the job is tough, we get tougher than the job."

—George Cullum, Sr.

So how exactly do you do this?

Ready, Set, Go!

First, when is it time to begin networking?

Now ... or better yet, *yesterday*!

It is easiest to begin networking when you don't have to do it. When recruiting others to help you isn't necessary and when there is no pressure to "get results" is when networking is easiest. Doing it for fun and to establish relationships with others just because you want to is the best time to begin networking.

How?

You may not even realize it, but you are probably already networking! Chatting with friends, coordinating your child's gymnastic meet, working at a job, etc., all of this is networking … getting in touch with others.

Excellent networkers can also be call *good socializers*. They are people who approach others at work, parties, during family reunions, at the bus stop … everywhere there are people. They chat about everything from the weather to their dog's obedience class to their business, and make it interesting for others to listen. They are continually establishing and furthering the relationships they have, and they do it all the time.

"The aim is not more goods for people to buy, but more opportunities for them to live."

—Lewis Mumford

You can do this. Talk to others about things that interest you, business or pleasure, and increase the number of people you meet. Get to know as many new people as possible, and maintain and enhance the relationships you have already. By socializing and talking to people you *are* networking. Not so hard, is it?

Networking Within

If you are currently employed, now is a great time to establish a rapport with people who are likely to become friends and who could someday be valuable business contacts. Get to know:

- people you work with
- customers you serve
- suppliers in your industry
- people who work for the competition
- personnel throughout your organization
- people working for the business next door
- the convenience store attendant

- the mail service people
- any and all other people who seem interesting or have interesting careers

 By getting to know as many people as possible, you increase your chances of knowing people who can help you when you need to find a job.

Changing jobs is very common in today's world, and many people tend to stick to similar sorts of occupations. The youth counselor may become a social worker, the gasoline truck driver a petroleum distributor, and the secretary an office manager. Occupations change, but the general field of work often stays the same.

 Even if you are changing to a completely different field of employment, the contacts you make can still be useful. People travel in many different circles, and you never know who will be able to help you.

The more people you know, the better your chances of knowing someone who can help you. Become a social butterfly and establish contacts who make your life interesting today and may help with your job search tomorrow.

The instrument supplier you met as a hospital nurse may also sell apparatus to the extended care facility you want to work in, and they may know people there. The workshop provider you met as a social worker may work for the company you now want to be hired by. The contacts you make today may come in handy when you are looking for work tomorrow. If you make a good impression now, searching for employment later will be easier.

Extracurricular Contacts

Your contacts outside of work can also be valuable networking connections. People you met at the new parent's workshop, the name after yours on the baseball league phone list, and members of the organic cooking club you belong to are all people you currently network with who could come in handy with your job search. Casual acquaintances now may become fruitful business contacts when looking for work at a later time.

 Never rule out the influence others can have on your job search. Assistance may come when you don't expect it from people you never expected could help. Network with everyone.

The key is to do things and meet people all the time. All people you meet and everyone you know can be helpful when you are searching for employment.

Searching for Opportunities

Be prepared and always be on the lookout for career boosters and chances to network. Missed opportunities will greatly increase the time it may take to fulfill your career change. Always be on the lookout for:

— "signs" that a business needs your services. Listen to the local business gossip to see if you can help out or fit in.

— "opportunities" to show themselves. Noting that a retail outlet is poorly laid out may be your chance to describe your management and organization experience.

— "people" who may be able to help you. Remember, never underestimate the influence someone may have on your employment situation. Network all the time.

"Problems are only opportunities in work clothes."

—Henry J. Kaiser

Always be prepared:

- for conversation. Talking with people is the crux of networking, and you must invest the time, energy, and enthusiasm to make your conversations interesting and useful. Possessing the "gift of gab" is essential.

- look, smell, and dress well at all times. Your appearance has a dramatic influence on the impression you make.

- carry a daily planner to keep track of important information your networking contacts provide.

- carry business cards and keep a copy of your resume in your car or briefcase. More importantly, pass them out to people you network with.

- speak to everyone you meet. Yes, everyone. Say hello to people you pass on the street and smile. Your positive outlook and pleasantries will be appreciated and remembered.

 The person you smiled at and greeted on the street yesterday may be the employer interviewing you today.

Always present yourself in the best light and you will be remembered and helped. People prefer to do good for good people.

The Etiquette of Networking

So, networking is telling all the people you meet and know everything about you that is wonderful, and they will help you get a job. What more is there to know?

Lots!

Effective networking is much more than simply regurgitating your skills, strengths, and assets to everyone you know and meet. It takes skill, technique, and lots of common sense.

"Think like a man of action, act like a man of thought."

—Henri Bergson

Suppose:

You are attending a family reunion, and a cousin you had lost contact with approaches you. You exchange pleasantries, and Cousin Ed begins telling you about his search for employment. He describes the jobs he has had and what he is looking for now. He provides you with an extensive description of all the skills he has ever used and then goes on to tell you about the volunteer work he is doing. He takes a deep breath and tells you where he is currently looking for work and finally ends by asking if you know of employers looking for help. You respond with a "no" without thinking so you don't inspire another 30-minute monologue. You quickly excuse yourself and realize Ed knows no more about you than when you met 30 minutes ago. This reunion stuff isn't as much fun as you thought it would be.

Then you meet Great Uncle Peter. You heard he was recently laid off, and with the experience of Cousin Ed painfully fresh, you try to dodge him. Thankfully, you don't succeed. Peter asks you about your life including your family, job, and holidays. After that opener, you have more interest in hearing about him. He tells you about his family and hobbies, and then mentions his recent layoff ... "Here we go," you think. To your surprise, Peter doesn't recite his resume, but briefly describes how he is considering turning a hobby into a job, and then asks what hobbies you enjoy. The discussion continues on in this casual two-way exchange, and by the end, you have provided Peter with the names of three people to contact and have made a mental note to keep an eye out for businesses looking for employees. Peter gives you his business card, and you leave reacquainted and eager to help.

"Good communication is as stimulating as black coffee, and just as hard to sleep after."

—Anne Morrow Lindbergh

This example illustrates the difference between effective and ineffective networking. You want people to *want* to help you, not just know everything there is to know about you. So how will you convey your skills and desires while maintaining a positive and useful exchange? Who must you talk to? What networking skills are necessary to become effective and productive? What are all the things you need to know to become a networker with etiquette?

Make it a personal goal to network with one new person every day. Steady work will ensure you maintain your momentum and stay active in your job search.

Knowing Who to Talk To

Who do you network with? Do you browse the yellow pages for company contact names, or do you ask your best friend? Do you involve family, friends, and casual acquaintances, or do you limit your networking to business associates? Is everyone fair game, or is there a limit? Just who are you supposed to be networking with?

Everybody!

"Don't wait for your ship to come in; swim out to it."

—Anonymous

Yes, everybody. If you want to be successful marketing your business (you), then you must tell everyone what you have to offer.

✔ When casually speaking with your hair stylist, let her know you are looking for work and in which occupation. She may tell you about a customer who was discussing how hard it is to find employees who have the qualifications you do.

✔ Tell your friends you are looking to change careers, and ask for their help. They are your friends because they like and admire you, and they will be great at passing on positive information about you.

✔ Call past business associates and meet with them for lunch. People you worked with, customers you served, suppliers you chatted with, and people who worked for the competition are all potential luncheon partners.

✔ Tell people who belong to the same model train club as you about your career plans and goals. Clubs and organizations you belong to are a great place to network because you already know the people.

✔ Join business and professional associations. This helps you stay in touch, hear the latest goings on in the industry, and maybe hear of job opportunities before they are finalized or advertised. You also have the perfect opportunity to network with people working in your industry.

✔ Take advantage of this time and join recreational clubs and organizations. While you're at meetings, get to know people and tell them what's going on in your life … that you're looking for work. You win two ways here: more networking opportunities and you have fun!

✔ Contact those whose business cards you keep so neatly in your rolodex. Ask them if they know of any openings within their companies that you could fill and for further ideas and suggestions. Those old business cards are good for more than just collecting dust.

✔ Discuss your plans for the future with Grannie Edith at the family gathering. With all the grandchildren she has, she just might know of someone who can help you out.

✔ Advise your financial planner that you will be stopping all retirement contributions until you locate employment and any ideas or suggestions she has would be welcomed. This will be sure to stimulate her thoughts and suggestions.

And so on …

Almost everyone can help with your job search, but you must initiate conversations and tell people what you need. Never underestimate the influence others can have on your job search.

Connecting with People

Perfect networking results in others networking for you. When an individual feels connected to you, he or she is more likely to remember you, remember what you say, and help you. By connecting positively with people and leaving a lasting impression of yourself, you encourage them to keep an eye open and to tell others about you.

 By recruiting others to network for you, you greatly improve your chances for success.

Establishing a strong positive connection with others should be one of your prime networking goals. You can find a job on your own, but it is a lot easier and more fun when you have others helping you out.

So, how do you establish this connection?

Paper Connection

Establishing a paper connection means allowing people to get to know you on paper: via your resume, business card, introductory letter, personal brochure, or any other written correspondence.

 For more information on these marketing tools, see **Job Hunting Made Easy**.

This could also include articles written about you, business correspondence, or any other written material where your name is mentioned.

A paper connection allows your name to briefly cross a person's mind, but the impression it leaves is usually minimal. Unless the information provided has a strong impact or is very creative and unique in its presentation, few people will remember your name, the information they read, and how both are connected.

 Paper tools are significantly more effective when you have connected with a person in a different way first. They are effective tools when used as reminders.

Telephone Connection

Contacting people over the phone allows them to become somewhat acquainted with you. You become a "person" rather than merely a list of skills on paper, and more of your personality comes through. Your voice makes you distinct, your telephone manners convey information about you, and your enthusiasm can be felt.

This type of connection is still limited. People get a sense of who you are but don't experience the "total you." Your telephone skills must be honed so you can portray information about your skills, your desires, and your personality in a way that is quick, concise, and interesting. You must rely on your voice to convey all the information about yourself that you want to convey.

 Practice mock telephone networking conversations with a friend. Ask him to provide feedback on how you sounded during the conversation and for suggestions on how to make yourself sound more convincing, enthusiastic, and knowledgeable.

Word-of-Mouth Connection

The next time your ears ring, it could be because others are talking about you … enjoy the sensation! When other people talk about you, the things you have done, and what you have to offer, you are connecting in a very strong way. Little else has as much of an impact as the first impression another person provides of you. Whether good or bad, what others think and say about you will greatly affect the people you are connecting with.

So, when people ask how they can help, suggest they tell others about you. Give people permission to describe your work habits, education, strengths, accomplishments, and personality to others. If they know of anyone who may be hiring or who knows of contacts that would help you, encourage them to talk about you in a positive way.

 Ask people to tell you when they have spoken with others about you. This allows you to follow up with a personal contact, making the impression of you even stronger.

The connections others make for you will be very profitable for your job search.

Personal Connection

Connecting with people personally is the most effective method of networking. People develop an impression of the whole you; your voice, your mannerisms, your face, your look, your enthusiasm, your voice, *and* the skills you have to offer.

In addition, people are usually more willing to give "people" time than words on a page or voices on a telephone. Therefore, you will have more time to network than if you simply call or leave a resume. Your impression will be much stronger and longer lasting when you personally connect with others.

One effective networking interaction is more effective and fruitful than several interactions done haphazardly.

The degree to which you connect with people involves more than simply how you contact them, but the method of contact will influence how much of an impact you make. Before you approach people consider how important it is to make a complete and lasting impression, then decide how you will contact them.

Speaking with Confidence

Communicating is much more than the words you say, it is your body, your eyes, your voice, and your emotions. *How* you say things has as much of an impact (usually more) than *what* you say. So be sure that when you network, you communicate totally.

Show your enthusiasm and allow your passions to come through when you speak. Let your body portray your confidence and excitement. Let your eyes portray your passions and knowledge. Allow your voice to paint a true picture of how you feel about what you say, and use descriptive words that portray your skills, knowledge, and eagerness. People will be more willing to listen when you speak with enthusiasm, and they will "hear" more.

"Flaming enthusiasm, backed up by horse sense and persistence, is the quality that most frequently makes for success."

—Dale Carnegie

In order to communicate totally, you must:

- *believe in the things you say.*
  If you don't believe what you say, why would anyone else?

- *be willing to speak.*
  If your parents taught you being seen but not heard was the way to be, then it's time for a new lesson. *Speak out and be heard!* Help people remember you.

Life is about being, feeling, and sharing. Allow your life to impact others and leave lasting impressions.

- *be real.*
  Don't worry about what other people will think. If you have an opinion, voice it. Let others discover the real you and know that you think about issues and have made informed opinions. Not voicing your opinions because you worry about what others will think accomplishes nothing. Be yourself and let the real you come out.

Being "silly" with enthusiasm or "bursting" with ideas indicates you are a thinker and a passionate person. These are very positive qualities.

Maintaining a Positive Outlook

Generally, people are drawn to positive, happy people and avoid those who are negative. Simple fact, but sometimes hard to internalize. Practice finding the good in all situations.

- You're unemployed … you have the opportunity to discover new career paths.

- Your last interview was a bomb … you can learn a lot about interviews and be more prepared next time.

- It's been raining for a week … the flowers are sure to bloom soon.

 Many of us are conditioned to see the negative in situations, but it is much more fruitful and enjoyable to do the opposite.

Life is a matter of perspective. It's your choice as to which perspective you choose.

When you are networking, be sure you emphasize the positive in all things you describe. People are much more willing to listen and help you when you describe yourself in a positive manner. Be conscious to convey positive descriptions, positive ideas, and a positive image of yourself.

How?

Replace: "I am looking for a better job."
with: "I am working at broadening my horizons and expanding my experience."

Replace: "I am a carpenter, but there aren't any jobs in the winter."
with: "I am a carpenter eager to work every season of the year."

Replace: "I have never been a service representative before."
with: "I know I would do a great job as a service representative because I enjoy working with people, I am fast, and I show people that I care."

Replace: "I am looking for work and haven't been able to find anything on my own. Can you help?"
with: "I would appreciate any ideas or suggestions you have that could increase my employment opportunities."

Your goal when networking is to encourage people to help you, not bore and depress them. Focus on the positive and be sure the words you say and how you say them leave a lasting, positive impression.

By being positive you will interest others, come across as someone worth helping, and you will feel better also. Changing your behavior works to change your attitude.

Listening and Following Through

The main reason for networking with people about your employment intentions is to obtain their assistance. When others demonstrate their willingness to help by providing suggestions, let them know their suggestions are valuable to you.

How?

– By listening. When you ask for help, listen to the answer. This is your chance to tap into another person's network and his or her job search ideas and skills. Take advantage of it.

– Being prepared.

✔ carry a notebook/daily planner and pen

✔ write down the businesses, names, phone numbers, and titles of people to whom you have been referred

✔ keep records of "who" provided you with "what" information

✔ carry business cards and resumes

✔ keep time free in your schedule to follow through on suggestions

Always have a supply of business cards on hand to give to the people you network with. These cards will be a reminder of your career goal, name, and phone number. (For more information on job hunting tools refer to **Job Hunting Made Easy**.)

Demonstrating how prepared you are is sure to impress those you speak with and encourage them to help you more.

– Follow up on the suggestions others have provided. Contact people to whom you have been referred, attend business meetings you were invited to, and use the suggestions and ideas provided. It is your networking *responsibility* to follow up on suggestions.

– Speak positively about suggestions. Even if you don't think an idea will work or that a suggestion is useful, listen anyway. Nothing stops people from helping you quicker than telling them their ideas aren't useful.

Even when a suggestion doesn't seem to be useful, follow through on it anyway. You never know when a door to employment will be opened.

– Ask people to continue talking. Many people will stop giving suggestions when they feel they have been speaking too much, not when they run out of ideas. It is up to you to encourage them to continue brainstorming and offering ideas.

– Encourage friends, family members, and/or business associates to talk about you with people they know. This is essential to getting your name out … quickly and effectively!

Always ask if you can tell "contacts" who referred you to them.

– Thank people for their time and effort. People do not have to help you and it is important you show your gratitude.

Remember, the suggestions and assistance others provide are the reason you are networking.

Notes of Appreciation

It is imperative you acknowledge the effort and thought others have given to your job search. Let them know their help is appreciated and that you welcome further suggestions by:

— thanking people for their suggestions and ideas.

— keeping them informed on what came of their suggestions, comments, ideas, and referrals.

— sending them thank-you cards, letters of appreciation, or other gestures of thanks.

Use thank-you cards to show your gratitude and as a further opportunity to network. Restate your career goal or note something you "forgot" to mention during your conversation.

By doing these things you show your gratitude and encourage people to continue "thinking" for you. Who knows, if this suggestion wasn't "the one," maybe the next one will be.

Paying for a networking lunch shows people you value the time and effort they have put into meeting with you ... and it makes them feel good. And making others feel good is what networking is all about.

Networking: A Two-Way Street

As much as your focus may be on yourself and what you want from your networking endeavors, remember that other people have lives and needs as well. The best way to encourage people to help you is to help them first.

"You can make more friends in two months by becoming more interested in other people than you can in two years by trying to get people interested in you."

—Dale Carnegie

Not only is this a good way to help your networking success, it is a good way to live your life. Help others and they will help you.

✔ When you know someone needs help, help him or her. Don't wait for the person to ask, simply do.

✔ When people do ask your assistance, provide it.

✔ Remember people's interests, hobbies, and unique personality characteristics. This way if you discover something about "underwater basket weaving" you can let your "weaver" contact know about it.

Good intentions are empty thoughts ... good deeds are cherished and remembered.

✔ Help others with small things. Small deeds added up are "worth" more than large deeds done sporadically.

✔ Do for others with the intent of doing good, not with the intent of receiving back.

While people may not expect anything in return when they help you out, a good deed returned will be appreciated and remembered.

Networking is more than simply encouraging people to help you find work, it is a way of life. Making contact with others in a positive and personal way will help you out in the long run and will be a rewarding way to live your life.

Practice

All these skills are meaningless unless you use them and use them well. Practice. Begin approaching others and using your networking skills. The more you practice, the better you will become … and the more rewarding your efforts will be.

"The worst sin towards our fellow creatures is not to hate them, but to be indifferent to them; that's the essence of inhumanity."

—George Bernard Shaw

In Summary

Effective networking is merely speaking with people about the things you do so as to leave a lasting positive impression on them. If you speak to many people about the things you want and leave them motivated to help you, then you will have networked effectively.

Schmooze without Sleaze

Helping others and requesting their assistance is perfectly acceptable and necessary in our society. We all rely on others to a certain degree in our lives, and this is a healthy social practice. The unhealthy practice comes when our helping relationship with other people becomes sneaky, one sided, or disrespectful. When this happens we are no longer networking, we are using.

"I shall tell you a great secret, my friend. Do not wait for the last judgment; it takes place every day."

—Albert Camus

Schmoozing is the respectful, considerate, and acceptable use of another person's skills, knowledge, and talents. It is networking know-how. When you sincerely describe what you want and need from others while maintaining honesty and integrity, then you are a proficient and respectable networker. This should be your goal.

Be cautious of "sleaze" seeping into your networking. You will know when it happens by that feeling in your gut that what you are doing is wrong (not uncomfortable or awkward as networking may be when you first begin, but *wrong*).

The old cliché "The ends justify the means" is a sleazy cliché. Remember that when you reach your goal you want to have friends to enjoy your success with you.

Some sleazy practices to avoid are:

- *Saying you will help someone and not following through.*
  You may trick someone into helping you once, but not twice. And you will leave a negative impression of yourself.

- *Lying to people.*
  This includes giving half truths and omitting necessary information. When you lie about yourself or your intentions you compromise your integrity and you will inevitably be caught in your lie. You risk hurting others and hinder your chances for employment.

"Knowledge without conscience is the ruination of the soul."

—Francois Rabelais

- *Pretending to be genuinely interested in a person's life as a way of getting information or help from him or her.*
  Be up front with people with your intentions and desires and they will respect your honesty. They may not be able to help, but the positive impression you leave will gain their respect. Who knows, maybe someday they will be able to help.

- *Contacting friends only when you need something.*
  Friends are people you have a relationship with that goes beyond simply helping each other out in times of need. If the only time you contact them is when you want something, you will discover your friendships ending. Ask friends for help, but keep up the casual part of your relationship as well.

- *Using a "you owe me" attitude.*
  We all have people who "owe" us a favor, but approaching them with a "you owe me" attitude will make them resentful and angry. They may feel obligated to help you this time, but be sure they will never help you or ask for your help again. Approach people in a respectful and cooperative manner.

- *Flirting.*
  Giving people the impression that you are "available" if they help you out is a dangerous practice. If they do help they may expect to be "paid" for their efforts, and this could lead to trouble … for you. Use your brain, creativity, and resourcefulness when networking, not sex.

Sleazy networking practices are ineffective, unfair, and often back-fire. They leave people with a bad feeling about you. Schmoozing, on the other hand, will help you make friends and find work. This is what positive networking is all about.

 "Six essential qualities that are the key to success: Sincerity, personal integrity, humility, courtesy, wisdom, charity."

—Dr. William Menninger

ummary

These are the fundamentals of networking: knowing when and where to begin, knowing about etiquette, and understanding the difference between schmooze and sleaze. You're well on your way, keep your chin up!

Chapter 4

Networking Know-How

Now down to the nitty gritty ... the networking "how to's." The things you will say, the approaches to take, and discovering how to keep your contacts working for you, this is networking "know-how."

"Wonder rather than doubt is the route of knowledge."

—Abraham Joshua Heschel

Opening-Line Bloopers

Some people may say that what you say isn't important, as long as you make the initial approach.

Not!

How you ask people for help is just as important as asking. Here are some opening-line bloopers to avoid.

1. "So, I heard you could get me a job. When do I start?"
   Probable Response: "How about never!"

2. I have a racquetball game in 30 minutes, so could you think of people I should contact quickly."
   Probable Response: "Sure ... I can't think of anyone."

3. "My mother told me I should talk to you."
   Probable Response: "Maybe she should hold your hand, too."

4. "You're my last resort for finding a job, can you help me?"
   Probable Response: "Man, are you desperate!"

5. "You don't know me, but I was wondering if you could help me locate a job?"
   Probable Response: "You're right, I don't know you, why should I?"

6. "Remember me, I met you at Mr. John's Restaurant before I was fired. I'm looking for work again, and I would like to talk to you."
   Probable Response: "If you were fired, why would I want to jeopardize my reputation by helping you?"

7. "Rebekah, remember the favor I did for you last month? Well, now I want to be repaid."
   Probable Response: "So I owe you, do I?! Well, I'm going to do just enough to repay you."

"Tact is the art of making a point without making an enemy."

—Howard W. Newton

 aying it Right

Knowing what to say and how to say it is an important part of networking ... and often the most intimidating part. Having an idea of what to say to people makes networking easier, enjoyable, and rewarding.

The Right Way ... Is There One?

"What do I say when I approach people?" This is one of the most common questions, but unfortunately there is no simple answer. The main reason is that every person is different. Each person who networks and each person he or she networks with necessitates a slightly different approach and different conversation. Therefore, to provide the exact words for you to say would make your job more difficult. You would be concentrating on how to "fit" a script into your conversation rather than listening to what the person had to say.

"People have one thing in common: they are all different."

—Robert Zend

The following suggestions will help you decide what and how much to say. The exact words you use will depend on who you are talking to and what the situation is, but some general information should make your job easier. The rest is determined by your personality, intuition, and common sense.

Introductions

The most important and challenging part of networking is knowing how to approach people. Introducing yourself is a skill to learn. Practice as much as possible to do it comfortably.

Control your destiny by taking a proactive approach to life. Make it your responsibility to meet people, try new things, and jump at opportunities.

When introducing yourself to people, it is important to:

- introduce yourself at the beginning of a conversation. While it is not impossible to state your name halfway through the conversation or evening, it is more awkward.

- ask for the person's name.

- offer to shake his or her hand.

- be prepared to begin the conversation. You introduced yourself, now continue talking to the person.

Very simple and straightforward suggestions, but important ones. Telling people your name and asking theirs begins the conversation in a positive and respectful way.

Introduction Pitch A:

"Hello, Terri Prat? My name is Jack Jones. My friend Sue Trapper was telling me you are an avid snowboarder, and I'm interested in trying it. Do you know of a good place to take lessons?"

 Networking begins by talking to people … about anything. Your conversation does not have to begin with your career or even focus on your job search to be an effective networking session.

Introduction Pitch B:

"Sheila Atkins? My name is Roberta Waylens. I've heard about the work you do with pharmaceuticals, and I was wondering if you had a few minutes to chat."

 Remember people's names. Write them down along with the topics you discussed in your daily planner. You will remember the person and his or her name better when you do this.

Introduction Pitch C:

"Excuse me, my name is Joel Wandler. I saw you landscaping outside a house on Belgravia Drive, and I am enthralled by the architecture of the building. Can you tell me what you know about its design?" (Remember to ask the person's name if he or she doesn't offer it.)

It is up to you to initiate contact with people you are interested in meeting. Do it and the rewards will begin.

Social vs. Business Talk

It is not necessary for you to discuss your employment situation with everyone you meet immediately, but it is a good idea to connect with each person. By becoming familiar with other people, their likes and dislikes, their hobbies and occupations, you open the doors for further discussions. It may not be until your second or third meeting that a discussion about your employment situation seems appropriate, and it is better to wait until then than to bombard a person with your employment "trivia" before he or she is interested in hearing it.

"Nothing is ever lost by courtesy. It is the cheapest of pleasures, costs nothing, and conveys much. It pleases him who gives and receives and thus, like mercy, is twice blessed."

—Eratus Wiman

Once it seems appropriate to approach a person about your job situation, it is important to maintain a personal feeling in your discussions. Casual conversation (the weather, a baseball game, the family, etc.) mixed with business talk keeps a discussion personal. Maintaining an appropriate "mix" can make the difference between encouraging people to help you or to avoid you.

So, how much casual vs. business talk should you engage in? Well, that depends on who you are talking to.

✔ *New acquaintances*
When you first meet people in a casual or social setting (vs. a business setting) you want to develop a personal rapport with them. The initial meeting is an opportunity to get to know the person; learn about the person's likes and dislikes, find out more about his or her family, and develop a friendship. After you develop a personal

connection and feel the time is right to begin "talking business," it is still a good idea to include a lot of casual conversation. Remember this new acquaintance has put his or her trust in you as a friend, and it is up to you to maintain the friendship.

Even if a new acquaintance cannot help you immediately, continue to develop your relationship. Your goal in networking is to meet lots of people and as a spinoff, find employment.

✔ *New business acquaintances*
When you contact people you want to do business with immediately (employers, people "in the business," people to whom you were referred, etc.) who are virtual strangers, it is best to keep the casual conversation to a minimum. When your intention is to obtain employment information or follow through on employment tips, use business conversation. Keep your networking conversation brief and to the point. Discuss your intentions and the skills you have to offer and ask about employment opportunities. Leave a strong positive image of yourself without taking up too much of their time.

Be considerate of others' time restrictions and needs. Using time people don't have causes them to resent you rather than help you.

✔ *Business contacts*
The people you met through previous employment (paid or volunteer) or who you know are "in the business" are your business contacts. These are not only previous employers and people you worked directly with, but also customers you served, suppliers you dealt with, employees of the competition, members of associations or affiliations you belong to, your best friend's uncle who's in human resources … everyone you had contact with in your employment or whom you know professionally.

It is essential to demonstrate networking savvy by including casual conversation in these discussions. You know these people and are familiar with the work they do (and maybe even their hobbies or families), so it is important your discussion have a personal element. Take time to reacquaint yourself with the person and then discuss your employment intentions. Finding employment will be the focus of your discussion, but adding a personal touch reminds people you are interested in them, and not just using them.

Drinking alcohol while networking over lunch is not a good idea. Alcohol dulls your perception and you don't want to convey to an employer that you can't make it through a business luncheon without a drink.

✔ *Casual acquaintances*
Take what you do with business acquaintances and flip the proportion of casual to business talk. Instead of a little personal and a lot of business, focus on personal issues with a little business added in.

People you are familiar with, for example your bank teller, your dentist, the babysitter's parents, the people you see at church, are all people you want informed about your job search. Mention your employment intentions, but remember to keep the conversation casual. If they have ideas for you then continue discussing and networking with them, but if they don't, letting them know your intentions has expanded the number of people who know about your job search by one. And this is the "one" who may hear about the perfect job for you!

Exception:

Like most rules, there is an exception to this one, too. If you know a casual acquaintance could be instrumental in helping you locate work, discuss your employment intentions with him or her in more depth. Use your casual discussion to set up the more formal networking meeting where you can further discuss your job situation.

Example:

"Mr. Robbins, this is Jane Claussen, how are you doing? I know you're in the electronics industry, and I will be looking for work when I graduate in June. Would you have some time to chat with me about the type of work your company does?"

Use the expertise others have, but use it wisely. Approach people who may potentially help you and recruit their assistance.

✔ *Relatives and friends*
Friends and relatives can be the key to your networking success. These are the people to whom you can really talk about your employment intentions. Tell them details about the work you want to do, and ask for their assistance. The better you know people, the more time you can spend telling them about the work you want.

Your best friend will want to know every detail, your CEO Aunt will need to know your skills. Your cousin Fred should know about your employment desires, and your good friend Mary should know of your credentials and experience. These are the people who are instrumental in helping you locate work. Network, network, network!

Gauge the amount of information you give relatives and friends by how close you are to them. The closer you are, the more interested they will be and the more potential there is for them to help you. Remember, a distant relative is more like a casual acquaintance than a close friend.

The amount of casual to business talk will vary from situation to situation. Use the suggestions provided only as a guide, and then let your heart, head, and common sense lead you.

Topics for Discussion

The topics you discuss will vary from person to person. Again, there is no "right" answer describing things to discuss under specific situations, you must "feel" the right answer. Use your intuition and knowledge of the other person to tell you what to say.

Remember to mix casual conversation with business talk when appropriate, but your employment networking focus is business. Some potential business networking topics for discussion are:

– your career objectives and jobs you are interested in.

– the skills you would like to use in your next job.

– the type of company you would like to work for.

– the aspects of previous jobs you enjoyed.

– the places where you have been submitting resumes.

– the people you have networked with thus far.

– your non-work-related skills that would be an asset to employers.

– anything else that seems to make sense.

Use tact and be sensitive. Speak and act without offending.

Remember to look for cues of interest and boredom and gauge your discussion accordingly. Choose the things you discuss depending on how much you believe it will impact the other person. Don't waste your time telling someone who doesn't really like you about your career plans and then forget to mention to your human resources friend that you are unemployed. Use your head.

Networking Scenarios

Again, memorizing "scripts" makes networking more difficult, as you will be concentrating on the script rather than what the person is saying. Of course, the other problem is that the person you are talking to doesn't have a copy of the script! Here are some examples just to give you an idea … don't memorize them.

"It isn't life that matters; it's the courage you bring to it."

—Hugh Walpole

Scenario: Requesting Favors

Now is the time to ask for favors. Contact people you suspect would be willing to help or who have in the past said "If you ever need anything, let me know" and recruit them. Let people help you out.

Networking Pitch A:

"John, how are you doing? How did things work out with the naturopath I referred you to? Did your daughter's allergies get any better?" …

"I'm not sure if you heard, but I'm looking for a career in the welding industry. I know you work with some welders and I was wondering if you know of any employers who might be looking for people to apprentice with them?" …

"Any other suggestions or ideas you have would be great. Thanks for all your help, and I hope your daughter's allergies continue to improve."

 People help out more when they do it for its own intrinsic value rather than out of a feeling of obligation.

If someone "owes" you a favor, it's not necessary to remind him or her. Casually bring up the situation where you helped the person, but don't make the person feel he or she owes you. You want people to help you because they want to, not because they have to. When people are asked to return a favor they may do so grudgingly, with a sense of obligation rather than genuine kindheartedness.

Describe your strongest skills, attributes, and experience as well as your knowledge and interest in a company when speaking with an employer. Be brief, to the point, and leave a positive impression.

BB

Scenario: Networking with Distant Acquaintances

Contacting people with whom you are loosely acquainted or whom you haven't spoken with in a long time is important. You want to encourage them to help you without feeling like you are using them.

Networking Pitch B:

"Lance, this is Bernie Phillips. It's been a long time since we've talked, how are things going?" …

"Lance, I'm not sure if you've heard, but my company recently downsized. I'm looking for work as a laboratory technician, but there are few positions available in my community. I know you used to work in a hospital in your state and was wondering if you know of any people I can contact." …

"I know it's hard to think of names on the spot, but thanks for trying anyway."

"Hey, do you ever come back this way? When you do, why don't we get together with a few of the gang and go out to a movie. It'd be great for us all to get together again. Call me and we'll arrange something. And, if you should think of anyone else I could contact in your state about finding work, could you let me know?" …

"Good talking to you, bye for now."

It is easy to begin the conversation casually, but the key element is to end the discussion on a personal note as well. This reminds people that you still value your relationship and are not simply using them.

Contact all the people who could help you with your job search, but keep in mind that your period of unemployment is temporary. You need people's help now, but want to maintain your friendship for much longer.

Scenario: Recruiting Casual Contacts

People you know only slightly can be awkward to contact, but also very helpful. Approaching them requires tact and courage. It's not easy to ask people you hardly know for help, but it is necessary.

Be sure to introduce yourself and remind the person of how you are acquainted. Don't leave him or her wondering, "Where do I know her from?"

Networking Pitch C:

"Mrs. Brown, I'm Todd Lee. We go to the same art class, and I've heard that you are a member of the local chamber of commerce. I recently graduated from college, and am interested in meeting people in the business world. I was wondering if it's possible to get an invitation to attend one of your meetings or if you know of people I could speak with about employment in the computer industry?" …

"Thanks for your help. My phone number is 555-9087, and I look forward to our meeting. I know it's unusual for someone from art class to be asking for your help in this way, and I appreciate all that you are doing. See you in class."

Be specific about what you want from people. Give them a place to begin helping you and then expand as appropriate.

Be sure that when you next see this person you approach him or her and chat, not necessarily about your job search, but to enhance your personal relationship. You will not only be developing a business relationship, but furthering your personal one, too.

Scenario: Enlisting the Help of Business Associates

Business associates are people who know how you work, know the business, and know who the valuable contacts are. These are people you must contact who will be essential to your job search.

Networking Pitch D:

"Virginia, this is Darcy Martin, we worked together at The Workshop Place. How are you doing?" …

"Virginia, I am on the market again as a workshop facilitator and am trying to find out which agencies currently need people. I thought that because you are still employed in the field you may have heard of agencies who are looking for people. Do you know of any?" …

"Great, I remember those people and will contact them. I was also wondering if you've heard of Best Corporation. I think they are new in the business and was wondering what their reputation is like." …

"Thanks for all your help. If you hear of anyone else who is looking I would appreciate if you could call me. My home phone number is 555-1212. Talk to you soon."

Keep business contacts alive by having lunch or even sending Christmas cards. Old business associates come in handy in current (and future) job searches.

People in the business will be "up" on who's hiring and who's not. Enlisting their help will keep you in touch.

Scenario: Contacting Employers

Employers are people you must contact. While it may be easier to contact employers you know, all employers in your field can provide valuable assistance.

Know what you want from employers before you call them. Prepare a list of questions before your meeting so you know what to say and ask.

Networking Pitch E:

"Mr. Gainsworth, my name is Judith Plantz, and I am a certified lactation consultant. I know your hospital is committed to supporting and educating new mothers, and I was wondering what sort of breastfeeding programs you have in place?" …

"These sound very interesting. I have 3 years experience in the field and find that women and babies need the assistance of knowledgeable caregivers. Does your facility currently have any positions available?" …

"May I leave you my resume, anyway? I am very interested in your facility and believe that if a position does open up, I could be an asset to your health center. Thanks for your time."

Let your enthusiasm and personality come through when speaking with employers. Many people are looking for work, so it is up to you to describe and convey to an employer how you would be good for his or her company.

Many potential scenarios exist. The thing to remember is that you can and should allow yourself to be spontaneous and discuss different things with different people. No two people are ever alike and no two conversations will be either. Keep your job search interesting and productive by speaking with many people from various walks of life.

olunteering

Volunteering is an excellent way to learn about an industry. As well as being interesting and fun, it is a productive way to network and an excellent way to locate employment!

*"We work not only to produce
but to give value to time.*

—Eugene Delacroix

But what about employers? Why would they want to take the time to train and teach you about the business? What's in it for them?

Lots!

There are many employer benefits to recruiting and making use of volunteers:

✔ Employers have extra people on staff … and they don't have to pay them!

✔ Employers can utilize a person's knowledge and expertise without having to provide extensive training or a complete orientation. The person will be there a short time and can discover things about the company at his or her own rate.

✔ Employers have the opportunity to "try a person out" and see how he or she fits in with the company.

✔ An employer has an experienced "someone" to contact when a paid position becomes available.

✔ If an employer hires a previous volunteer, the company will not have to spend as much time orienting him or her to the firm and its procedures and practices.

So, there are benefits for the employer, what about you?

✔ You get to try a company out to see if you like working there.

✔ You expand your networking contacts to include:

– the employer for the company,

– the people you worked with,

– the customers you served,

– other employers you heard of,

– other people to whom you have been referred while volunteering,

– people you see in the building who work for other companies, etc.

✔ You keep your skills current. A related volunteer position keeps you in touch with your profession.

✔ Your resume is filled with volunteer positions instead of gaps that convey to employers that you were inactive.

✔ You maintain your momentum.

 One of the biggest momentum destroyers is sitting idle. If you remain active and continue to do things while you are unemployed, you will be less likely to fall into an idle "rut."

✔ You have the flexibility to continue looking for work with other employers and take days off when necessary.

✔ You have the opportunity to try new skills or use old ones in a new environment.

✔ You have the opportunity to establish a working relationship with the employer. Employers are more likely to keep you in mind for future positions and let business associates know about you when they are looking for an employee.

✔ You are more likely to be hired by a company if you have worked there. Showing your positive work ethic and demonstrating your skills makes you a resource to the company, one likely to be contacted when a paid position arises.

There are other ways you benefit from volunteering. Many people who volunteer discover they receive much more from their experience than they imagined. Some of these fringe benefits are:

✔ Regular contact with other people. This is perfect for your need to socialize and the necessity to network.

✔ The development of friendships with those you volunteer with.

✔ A feeling of achievement, accomplishment, and fulfillment.

✔ A sense of purpose and something to ground you when your days may otherwise run together.

✔ A way to productively fill your time.

✔ A true sense of giving and pride that you are doing things for the good of it, rather than for a fee.

✔ The rewards come from the results of your labor, not from money.

Take advantage of this time when searching for employment. Discover more about who you are.

Volunteering is a great way to expand your network, increase your chance of locating employment, and discover more about yourself. You win, the employer wins, everyone benefits from volunteer work.

Now is your chance to dedicate some of your time to volunteering. Plan for it and do it.

Timing

While it may seem the thing to do is to go out and find a volunteer position immediately, give yourself time to consider things before committing yourself. Is the time right for you to offer your services?

"Every calling is great when greatly pursued."

—Oliver Wendell Holmes, Jr.

The time to volunteer may be when:

✔ you know a company will be hiring employees in the near future. If you are interested in working for the company and would like to increase your chance of being chosen for a position, then offer your skills for free to show the employer your stuff. Your name, work habits, and the impression you make will be fresh in the employer's mind when the search for a paid employee begins.

✔ you believe you may be hired by company XYZ. Now is an excellent time to offer to help the company out for a brief period of time.

✔ you would like to try out a new occupation to "see how it feels" before committing to making a career change.

✔ you feel you need to be productive and keep active.

✔ you want to meet new people.

✔ you discover an organization or cause that parallels your morals and values. Volunteer for the good of it, to help out and to promote things you believe in.

Some volunteer positions may not lead to paid employment but will be of significant intrinsic value to you. And as a spinoff you may meet someone who can help with your job search.

Avoid volunteering if:

✔ you are new at being unemployed and are finding it a highly emotional and stressful time. You want to let your potential future employer know what a great employee you are, not how much you wish you still had your previous job. Take some time to adjust first.

✔ you are fresh out of work and just beginning to research careers and occupations. Wait until you choose a career path before committing yourself to any organization.

Choosing a Career Made Easy can help you to make a career decision you will be pleased with.

✔ you feel resentful in any way about offering your skills for free. No matter how impressive your skills, your attitude will come through and turn an employer off. If you can't be positive when volunteering, don't do it!

✔ you don't have the time to commit. If you are too busy to put in the time, don't offer to do it. Doing this will only succeed in leaving a negative impression.

Good timing will aid in your ability to leave a positive impression on an employer. Poor timing could cloud this impression. Choose the right time.

Identifying Opportunities

Locating a company to volunteer with is a task that should overlap with your job search. To maximize networking opportunities, the company you volunteer with should be connected to the industry where you want to work. After you have decided on a career path, have potential occupations in mind, and have identified potential companies to work for, then you are in a position to begin volunteering.

"There is no future in any job. The future lies in the man who holds the job."

—Dr. George Crane

The bottom line is that any company you would consider working for is a potential volunteer opportunity. It is up to you to determine:

✔ with which organization you would like to leave a positive impression

✔ in which company you would be most likely to be hired

✔ which business has the best connections

✔ which company you would most like to work for

Discovering a company to volunteer for should be a by-product of your job search networking, not a separate and different task. Remember, volunteering is supposed to make your job search easier, not more difficult.

Now choose the company you would feel comfortable volunteering for and go for it. Keep trying until you locate a company that jumps at the opportunity to have you.

There are organizations that you feel strongly connected to due to their purpose and mission. Volunteering for these organizations may not lead to employment but still allows you to meet new people and to network. Other volunteers may have similar ideals and values as you, and may thus have similar occupations. These are perfect people to network.

Approaching Employers

After you do your usual networking and have decided you would like to improve your potential for employment with an organization, then you can discuss volunteer opportunities with the employer.

Setting up a volunteer position is an extension of the networking you have already done.

Approach employers knowing what you have to offer and how their company will benefit. Be enthusiastic and convey to the employer that your desire to help the company is genuine. Let the employer know you will do a top notch job.

Before you approach an employer you must know:

• how much time you are willing to commit to volunteering, i.e., how many hours per day, days per week, and total weeks.

• in which capacity you would be willing to help out.

• that the company may not accept your request to volunteer. Even if the employer doesn't accept your offer, he or she will still be impressed by your willingness to help, and will remember it.

Set up a meeting to discuss your desire to volunteer and impress the employer so much that they can't possibly refuse your offer!

Volunteer Pitch A:

An organization you want to work for that has no positions currently available.

"Mr. Casey, I believe your organization possesses integrity and vision and would really like to join your team. I know your company is extremely busy, and I would like to help out by volunteering a few hours per week for a month. I am a talented draftsperson and would be willing to help you out in any related capacity."

Volunteer Pitch B:

An organization you want to work for that has an opening available.

"Ms. Nova, I understand that one of your secretaries left last month, and I can imagine the work is beginning to pile up. I have applied for the paid position, but I would also be willing to come in for the next two days to help you to catch up. I am a reliable individual and would like to help you out."

Volunteer Pitch C:

An organization you believe has integrity but holds little potential for employment.

"Mr. Rice, I believe strongly in what your organization does and know your current volunteers possess a commitment and passion similar to mine. I would like to offer my services in any way to help meet your organizational goals and further the impact you have on society. I am available three hours per week for as long as you need me."

 Even though your goals for "personal belief" volunteering may not be employment related, the people you meet and contacts you make are still worth it.

You never know whether an employer will accept your offer unless you try. Even if he or she doesn't, you have still left a strong impression of yourself by demonstrating your desire and willingness to help the company. This will not go unnoticed.

Volunteer Networking

Once you have established a volunteer position and are working for an organization, use your time effectively. This is the time to show your stuff and take advantage of networking opportunities. Leave a positive image of yourself by:

✔ *impressing the people you volunteer with and for.*
The only thing better than telling people what a great employee you would make is to show them. Give to your volunteer work the same dedication, commitment, energy, and enthusiasm you would a paid position.

✔ *networking with the people you volunteer with.*
Let them know about your plans, career goals, and employment desires. Treat each person you meet as a potential employer and make your networking pitch.

✔ *getting to know as many people in the industry as possible.*
Ask for the names of other employers and get to know the people with whom you do business. Meet the customers, consultants, merchants, clients, and anyone else you come into contact with. You can expand your network incredibly when volunteering.

✔ *helping out while not allowing yourself to be used.*
While volunteering is a great way to demonstrate your skills and abilities, be sure that your thorough and endless work does not eliminate the paid position you could have had.

Volunteer enough to show what a wonderful employee you would make. Lengthy or complex projects should be completed by paid staff, not a volunteer.

Exception: If you are volunteering for an organization run solely by volunteers, then feel free to take on a larger task.

Include information about all the volunteer work you have done in your resume.

✔ *knowing when enough is enough.*
Volunteering for the purpose of securing employment should be a temporary commitment. Before volunteering, provide the employer with a time frame in which you will help out, a couple of days to a couple of months depending on the type of work you will be doing. Remember, your goal is to provide an employer with a "flavor" of your work and you the opportunity to network further. Once these goals are fulfilled, it is time to move on.

Use this time effectively and it will be a rewarding experience.

Leaving Permanent Reminders

Before you complete your volunteer work leave permanent reminders of you so the employer remembers the effort and time you put in.

How?

✔ *Leave your resume.*
Thank the employer for allowing you the time to help out and demonstrate your skills and state your interest in a paid position. Leave a resume with a cover letter that outlines your skills and abilities and reminds the employer of your volunteer time.

Example

Dear Ms. Farlow,

The past three weeks I have spent helping out XYZ Company have been exciting, and I appreciate the opportunity to work with you. I believe I have much to offer your company and would like to be considered for any paid editorial positions that come available.

(Continue briefly describing the skills and experience that would make you an asset to the company.)

Enthusiastically,

Joe Schlitzer

Cover Letters Made Easy provides more examples of cover letters with impact and power.

✔ *Leave your business card.*
Every person you networked with should have a copy of your business card to keep your name fresh in their minds. There is nothing worse than discovering someone heard of a great position for you but didn't know your phone number.

✔ *Leave a farewell impression.*
Buy the people you worked with muffins on your last day or leave a bouquet of flowers. Show your appreciation and gratitude.

 People remember nice gestures because they are so rarely done. Take advantage of this and make it your personal goal to always leave a lasting positive impression.

✔ *Return to visit.*
After you have finished volunteering remind people you are still around. Mark in your calendar one day every month when you will visit the office. Continue doing this at least until you secure paid employment or longer if you really enjoy your visits.

Ensure your hard work volunteering and establishing contacts is remembered and used. Add the people you "worked" with to your ever increasing list of networking contacts, and keep them on your active list by remaining in contact with them. Establishing contacts is the first step, keeping them active is the key.

In Summary

While it is important to give 110 percent of yourself while volunteering, do not expect to be hired immediately (or at all) by the company you volunteered for. Your goal should be to establish lasting positive networking contacts who will assist you with your job search. Being hired by the company is a bonus.

Volunteering can result in developing many potentially influential networking contacts. Use your time wisely and volunteer for organizations you are really interested in.

"Greatness lies not in being strong, but in the right use of strength."

—Henry Ward Beecher

Maintaining Active Contacts

Establishing contacts and the initial "sell" is only the first step in effective networking. The real key is for these people to continue working for you. The proficient networker makes it a priority to keep contacts alive and working for him or her and this requires persistence, tact, and a commitment on your part.

It is more effective to keep established networking contacts "active" than to be continually making new ones.

How?

Keeping contacts alive is like managing a business. You must make sure your "employees" continue to be productive (continue helping you with your job search) by creating a positive "work" environment. You can rely on a few patent approaches when making the initial contact with people, but maintaining contacts requires additional thought and creativity.

 The benefits of maintaining contacts far outweighs the effort.

The Usual Probes

There are several "management" techniques you can use to keep your contacts working for you. Like managing any business you want to:

• keep people aware of their "jobs,"

• maintain a positive working environment, and

• keep the lines of communication open.

What this means when managing your networking contacts is:

• people need to know you still require their assistance,

• people's assistance is needed, appreciated, and desired, and

• you welcome people's suggestions, ideas, or contacts.

How you do this requires thought.

 "By perseverance the snails reached the ark."

—Charles Haddon Spurgeon

Maintenance Pitch A:

"Janet, thank you for giving me Ms. Smith's name and telephone number last month. I had a very positive discussion with her and she gave me the name of two companies to contact. I really appreciate you helping me out. If you should have any other ideas, please let me know. Oh, I did give you my business card, didn't I?

Maintenance Pitch B:

… "I'm glad to hear your job is going so well, Brittany. My job search is coming along. Like I told you before, I'm looking for work as a computer programmer and am amazed at how tight the job market is. However, I have received a few good leads from talking to people like yourself and believe the job for me is waiting around the corner …"

"Tell me more about the project you are involved in."

Maintenance Pitch C:

"Julie, this is Jeff Andrews, we met last month at the ham radio meeting. Julie, I remembered you saying you belonged to another radio club in a different county. I was wondering if I could get the name and phone number of the contact person there?" ...

"Like I told you, I am keen on getting to know as many people involved with ham radios, mainly because I love radios, but also because I am in the electronics industry and am looking for work. Thanks for the names, and if you know of any other clubs in the state, I would appreciate it if you could let me know. My number is 555-0099. Thanks again."

Maintenance Pitch D:

(A thank-you note)

Dear Ms. Grabinsky,

Thank you for taking the time to listen and brainstorm with me about potential employers looking for artists. I have contacted many of the people we discussed and the response has been very good. If you have any further ideas or suggestions, I would appreciate your calling me at 555-0036.

Thanks again,

Sarah Parsons

You get the idea ...

The usual probes consist of continuing to let people know that you are looking for work and that you appreciate their help. By contacting people regularly and maintaining a professional, considerate, and positive relationship, you keep your contacts alive ... and working for you.

"We're all born under the same sky, but we don't all have the same horizon."

—Konrad Adenauer

Creative Management

There is much more to contact management then simply the "reminder" techniques. The interesting (and effective) management comes when you really begin thinking about people you made contact with and putting your knowledge of them to use. Being personal makes people's connection with you even stronger.

Creative Maintenance A:

In a previous meeting with John Banks, a human resources manager, you discovered he enjoys spectator sports. You were given tickets to a local hockey game but cannot attend and decide to pass them on to John.

"Mr. Banks, when we were chatting about my career goals last month you mentioned you enjoy sports. I know this may seem a bit odd, but I was given two tickets to our local hockey game and cannot attend. I was wondering if you would like to use them."

By learning things about other people (and noting them) you open the door to help them out. And helping others out is the best way to encourage people to help you.

Creative Maintenance B:

"Ms. Jackson, there's a great windsurfing special on "Sports World" next Tuesday that I've seen before. I remembered that you love windsurfing and wanted to make sure you knew about it."

It is not necessary to mention your job search every time you speak to a person. If you continue to remind them that you are around and periodically mention you are still looking for work, people will remember.

Creative Maintenance C:

"John, you said you have your own home business. I recently met someone who could use your services. Would you like her number so you can contact her?"

Helping others is the best way to encourage them to help you.

Creative Maintenance D:

"Sarah, when we last met you were looking for work as a photographer. Are you still looking? …"

"I know an employer who is looking for someone with your skills, would you like his name and phone number?"

If you want to get to know someone better, set up a second encounter. Do it soon enough that the person will remember you from the first time.

Simply reconnecting is a great way of maintaining contacts.

Creative Maintenance E:

"Hi Jordan, this is Jake McKenzie, we met last week at the basketball game. I had such a great time talking to you I was wondering if you'd like to go to the game this week?"

Now you have a couple hours to chat. Talk about your employment situation but remember to make your appointment as interesting as your initial meeting. Business talk will grow out of casual talk, but should not smother it.

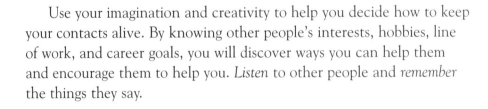

Use your imagination and creativity to help you decide how to keep your contacts alive. By knowing other people's interests, hobbies, line of work, and career goals, you will discover ways you can help them and encourage them to help you. *Listen* to other people and *remember* the things they say.

Conclusion

Don't wait for others to provide you with the things you want and need in life.

Networking well can take you down many roads. The worst case scenario is that you make a lot of friends along the way. The best case scenario is that you find a job *and* make a lot of friends.

 "It is a rough road that leads to the heights of greatness."

—Lucius Annaeus Senecad